G000067640

Photography by Will Heap

Kyle Cathie Limited

THE **FESTIVE** FOOD OF Italy

BY MADDALENA BONINO

First published in Great Britain in 1991 by
Kyle Cathie Limited
122 Arlington Road
London NW1 7HP
general.enquiries@kyle-cathie.com
www.kylecathie.com

ISBN 1 85626 678 8
ISBN (13-digit) 978 1 85626 678 9

Designed by **pinkstripedesign.com**

Photography by **Will Heap**

Illustrations by **Sally Maltby**

Picture research by **Sharon Tagg**

Home economy by **Annie Nichols**

Styling by **Roisin Nield**

Production by **Sha Huxtable & Alice Holloway**

Maddalena Bonino is hereby identified as the author of this work in
accordance with Section 77 of the Copyright, Designs and Patents
Act 1988.

A Cataloguing in Publication record for this title is available from the
British Library.
Reproduction by Colourscan Pty Limited
Printed and bound in China by SNP Leefung Printers Limited

pages 5–6: Green olives, Rainer Ohligschlaeger/zefa/Corbis

CONTENTS

SAN SILVESTRO

NEW YEAR'S EVE

Saint Silvester, to whom the last day of the year is dedicated, was Pope in the fourth century during the reign of Constantine, and contributed to making Christianity a recognised faith legalised by the emperor. New Year's Eve is a festival when secular and religious rites combine. Janus, the two-faced god, gives his name to the first month of the year as he can look both backwards and forwards, and this is the time when people sum up the results of the past year and look to the future. On the stroke of midnight windows are opened and fireworks light up the sky. The floor is swept of old dust, and in the south the more drastic measure is taken to break with the past by throwing out of the window broken crockery, pots and pans, and sometimes even furniture.

Grand dinners are organised; traditionally fish will appear as one of the courses, and stuffed pig's trotter served with lentils, which symbolise coins and are said to bring wealth if eaten on this day.

left Elena Segatini/Iconica/Getty Images

Gnocchi di Patate al Sugo

POTATO DUMPLINGS
WITH TOMATO SAUCE

1kg floury potatoes
225g plain flour, plus flour
   for dusting
pinch of salt
1 quantity tomato sauce (below)
100g grated parmesan

serves 4

1 Boil the potatoes in salted water until tender. Peel and mash while still hot, turn onto a floured surface, sprinkle with half the flour and season with the salt. Mix to a soft, slightly sticky dough, incorporating the rest of the flour.

2 Shape the dough into rolls the thickness of a thumb and cut into 2cm pieces. Roll each piece on the prongs of a fork or the side of a grater to mark them (this will ensure faster and more thorough cooking).

3 Drop each gnocchi on a floured tea towel, making sure the gnocchi do not touch each other or they will stick.

4 Cook the gnocchi, a few at a time in boiling water, for 5–8 minutes. Remove with a slotted spoon to a warm serving dish and ladle a little warmed sauce over each layer.

5 When all the gnocchi are cooked, finish with the remaining sauce and sprinkle with the Parmesan.

TOMATO SAUCE

1 small carrot, finely chopped
1 small onion, finely chopped
1 stalk of celery, finely chopped
2 tablespoons olive oil
400g tin plum tomatoes, chopped
2 bay leaves
1 teaspoon caster sugar
115g butter, cut into cubes
salt and freshly ground
   black pepper

1 Fry the carrot, onion and celery in the oil until just coloured, add the tomatoes, bay leaves, seasoning and sugar. Simmer until the vegetables are tender.

2 Depending on how you like your sauce, either pass the vegetables through a sieve and then incorporate the butter for a smooth sauce or simply add the butter and leave chunky.

SESAME NOUGAT

200g honey
250g sesame seeds
50g caster sugar
75g whole almonds, roasted
  and chopped
2 tablespoons almond oil
  or sunflower oil

1 Melt the honey over a low heat, add the sugar and bring to the boil, stirring constantly.

2 Add the sesame seeds and, still stirring, boil for 5 minutes. Add the almonds and cook for a further 5–10 minutes until the mixture feels denser.

3 Pour the mixture preferably onto an oiled marble surface, or any cold surface, and flatten with an oiled rolling pin while still hot.

4 Leave to cool a little, then with a sharp knife score into squares or diamonds and leave to cool. Stored in an airtight tin in a cool dry place, the nougat will last for a few months.

PESCE ARROSTO

ROAST FISH

Any type of fish on the bone can be used for this recipe:
for example brill, turbot, monkfish or sea bass.

75ml olive oil
2 mullets, together weighing
    about 1kg scaled and gutted
3 tablespoons balsamic vinegar
    or white wine vinegar
115g each of stoned green olives
    and capers
small bunch of flat-leaf parsley,
    finely chopped
salt and freshly ground
    black pepper

serves 4

1 Sprinkle 2 tablespoons of the olive oil into a roasting tray, arrange the fish in it, sprinkle with the remaining oil, half the vinegar, all the olives and capers, and season.

2 Bake in a preheated oven, 200°C/400°F/gas 6, for about 30 minutes, depending on the thickness of the fish.

3 Place the fish on a serving dish and keep warm. Reduce the cooking juices for a few seconds, add the remaining vinegar and the parsley and pour over the fish.

Sagra del Mandorlo in Fiore

FEAST OF THE FLOWERING ALMOND TREE

While the rest of Italy is still in the grip of winter, Sicily is celebrating the thaw and the coming of spring, heralded by the blossoming of the almond trees. During the first ten days of February a festival is held at Agrigento, a beautiful piece of countryside scattered with Greek ruins, almond trees and orange groves, in conjunction with a festival of folklore; while traditional dancers and singers show off their talents in the open air using the Greek amphitheatre as a stage, visitors sample the region's delicacies and enjoy the spectacle, surrounded by the scent of flowering almond trees.

The eighteen varieties of almond grown in Sicily are a fundamental ingredient in the local cuisine and in the preparation of celebratory dishes, which still reflect a strong Arab influence, especially in the use of honey, nuts and spices, and in the elaborate preparation involved. The time-consuming job of preparing some of these feast sweets fell at one time to the nuns, who it was thought would have sufficient time to make them. Martorana Fruit is one example, taking its name from a convent near Palermo, where the nuns still prepare marzipan, shape it and paint it to resemble all sorts of fruit and vegetables. During the fourteenth century this activity was temporarily halted in some convents by the religious authorities, as the nuns were neglecting their spiritual duties in favour of constructing these delicious sweets.

left Flowering almond tree, Inga Spence/Visuals Unlimited/Getty Images

FIORE DI MANDORLO

ALMOND BISCUITS

These 'Flowers of Mandorlo' are so called because of the shape they take on while cooking.

450g ground almonds
225g caster sugar
125g honey
1 teaspoon ground cinnamon
grated zest of 1 lemon
1 or 2 egg whites
icing sugar to sprinkle

makes about 30 biscuits

1 Mix together the ground almonds, sugar, honey, cinnamon and lemon zest with enough egg white to make a firm paste. Knead until smooth.

2 Shape into rounds and bake on a greased tray in a preheated oven, 150°C/300°F/gas 2, for about 20 minutes.

3 Leave to cool, then sprinkle with icing sugar.

CARNEVALE

The days before Ash Wednesday are eagerly awaited throughout Italy, as every village and town prepares to celebrate the annual Carnevale. Each carnival has a distinct character, celebrating a town or village's own historical connections, and some of the larger ones are well known, attracting visitors from all over the world. The oldest and best known is probably that of Venice, during which the whole city comes alive with masked and costumed revellers parading and processing through Venice's maze of streets.

A very different carnival takes place in Viareggio, in Tuscany, where gigantic floats and papier-mâché caricatures of public figures form a spectacular procession through the town's streets. In Ivrea, in Piedmont, the festivities commemorate the town's insurrection and end of feudal tyranny; after four days of costumed pageants and processions the insurrection is re-enacted, using oranges as ammunition. All ends well in the town square, where everyone meets to enjoy a rich and filling bean stew, La Fagiolata, the last over-indulgence before the restrictions of Lent.

left Versilia Vareggio Carnival, Tuscany; SIME/Corbis
right Viareggio; Marconi di Lauro/Stringer/Getty Images

FAGIOLATA

BEAN STEW

Italian sausages (*cotechini*) can be added to this rich stew; boil these separately, slice and add in the last 10 minutes of cooking.

550g dried borlotti beans
  soaked overnight
450g belly of pork,
  cut into cubes
1 large onion, diced
50g butter
2 tablespoons olive oil
450g ripe tomatoes (plum
  tomatoes if possible), roughly
  chopped
2 bay leaves
sprig of thyme
salt and freshly ground
  black pepper

serves 6

1 Put the soaked beans, pork belly and onion in a pot, cover with water and bring to the boil. Simmer until the beans are soft.

2 In a frying pan heat the butter and oil; when sizzling add the tomatoes, bay leaves and thyme, and cook for a few minutes.

3 Drain the beans and return to the pot with the tomato mixture. Simmer for another 30 minutes and adjust the seasoning. Serve hot with bread or polenta.

CHIACCHIERE

GOSSIPS

These traditional carnival sweets vary from region to region, and are known variously as *cenci* (rags), *nodi* (knots), *sfrappole* (bits and pieces), and so on. Grappa is sometimes used instead of Marsala, and lemon rind, cinnamon and aniseed can be added for a different flavour. They are all delicious, especially when served with a glass of sweet or sparkling wine.

450g plain flour, and extra
   for dusting
100g caster sugar
50g butter, softened
3 eggs
50ml Marsala
1 teaspoon vanilla essence
oil for deep-frying
icing sugar for sprinkling

1 Sift the flour into a bowl, make a well in the centre and add the sugar, butter, eggs, Marsala and vanilla. Mix well to form a dough. Turn out and knead on a floured surface until smooth.

2 Roll out thinly with a rolling pin or pass through a pasta machine until the dough is as thin as a sheet of lasagne. Cut the dough into strips.

3 Heat the oil in a deep frying pan and, when very hot, fry a few strips at a time until golden. Remove with a slotted spoon and drain on kitchen paper. Sprinkle with icing sugar.

right Venice carnival; Guenter Rossenbach/zefa/Corbis

EASTER

Easter is the most important feast in the religious calendar and is celebrated widely as a religious and secular festival. The word Pasqua derives from the Jewish Pasch-Passover, and indeed Easter is a time of transition from winter to spring, from the preparations and restrictions of Lent into the rejoicing and celebration of the Resurrection. Lamb, eggs and wheat always feature in Easter meals, lamb representing Christ, and also symbolising spring, the egg being the secular symbol of life and wheat the symbol of resurrection. In some parts of Italy it is still customary for farmers to take lambs and wheat to church on Good Friday to be blessed.

During the last week of Lent all sorts of special sweets and cakes are eaten; every region has its own speciality, but marzipan or chocolate reclining lambs bearing Christ's flag of victory can be found in all patisseries, as are *colombe*, dove-shaped cakes similar to Panettone, Pastiera Napoletana, a delicious cake which includes cooked wheat, fresh ricotta and orange candied peel, and of course chocolate eggs.

Easter Monday (Pasquetta) is traditionally spent picnicking in the warm spring air, with family and friends; in town or in country, good company and plenty of wine are all that are needed, and of course good simple Italian picnic food: vegetable, meat and pasta pies, cheeses, hams and sausages, breads, pizzas and focaccias.

right Easter Sunday in Caltagirone, Sicily; SIME/Corbis

AGNELLO BRODETTATO

LAMB WITH EGG AND LEMON SAUCE

3 tablespoons olive oil
1 large onion, finely sliced
85g Parma ham, diced
freshly ground black pepper
½ teaspoon grated nutmeg
1kg shoulder or leg of lamb,
   cut into cubes
4 tablespoons plain flour
250ml lamb stock
150ml dry white wine
3 egg yolks
juice of 1 lemon
small bunch of parsley,
   finely chopped

serves 6

1 Heat the oil in a saucepan and add the sliced onion and diced ham. Season with plenty of pepper and the nutmeg.

2 Toss the cubed lamb in the flour, add to the onion and ham and fry gently until all the pieces are golden.

3 Pour in the stock and simmer until almost evaporated, then add the white wine, season with a little more pepper, cover and leave to simmer for about 2 hours.

4 Lift the lamb pieces out of the saucepan, place in a serving dish and keep warm.

5 Whisk the egg yolks and lemon juice and stir into the cooking juices away from the heat. Pour over the lamb, sprinkle with chopped parsley and serve immediately.

TORTA PASQUALINA

EASTER PIE

Traditionally there are thirty-three pastry layers in this Ligurian pie, one for each
year of Christ's life; each layer is brushed with a feather dipped in oil, and then air
is blown between the layers with a straw to help the pastry rise.

1kg beet leaves or spinach
115g fresh breadcrumbs
250ml milk
10 eggs
200g grated parmesan
550g fresh ricotta
3 sprigs of fresh marjoram
225g butter
20 sheets of filo pastry
salt and freshly ground
   black pepper

serves 6–8

1 To make the filling, quickly blanch the beet or spinach leaves,
drain well and squeeze out all excess water, then chop finely. Mix
together the breadcrumbs and the milk and then stir in four of the
eggs, half the grated parmesan, the ricotta, the chopped leaves and
marjoram. Season and set aside.

2 Melt two thirds of the butter. Lightly grease a 24cm loose-bottomed
cake tin. Line with a sheet of filo and brush with melted butter; lay
nine further sheets over the first, brushing each one with melted butter
and taking care to cover the tin's sides.

3 Fill the cake tin with the mixture. Make six pockets in the mixture
and into each put a dot of butter and break an egg, then sprinkle
with the remaining parmesan and season.

4 Cover with the remaining ten sheets of filo, brushing each layer
with butter. Trim off the excess.

5 Bake in a preheated oven, 180°C/350°F/gas 4, for about
1 hour, and serve warm or cold.

SAGRA DEL CARCIOFO

FESTIVAL OF THE ARTICHOKE

The artichoke is native to Italy, becoming popular around the time of the Renaissance, when it made frequent appearances at the banqueting tables as both an ingredient and as a decorative centrepiece. Nowadays artichokes are grown and eaten in great quantity, cooked or eaten raw tossed in parmesan and good olive oil.

During April and May dozens of villages across Italy celebrate the harvest of the artichoke, when the crops are taken in large crates and boxes to the market square where they are praised for size and quality; some find their way into large frying pans to be offered with other local favourite specialities, where for the over-indulgent a glass of Cynar, a digestive made from the juice of artichokes, might be the order of the day.

FRIED ARTICHOKES

8 small artichoke hearts,
 trimmed and quartered (keep
 in water and lemon juice)
350g plain flour
2 eggs, beaten
olive oil for frying
2 lemons
salt and freshly ground
 black pepper

serves 4

1 Drain and pat dry the artichoke hearts. Toss in seasoned flour, then dip in the beaten egg.

2 Heat some olive oil in a frying pan and fry a few pieces of artichoke at a time, turning occasionally, until golden. Drain on kitchen paper and serve hot with lemon wedges.

ARTICHOKES ROMAN-STYLE

8 small or 4 large artichokes
bunch of flat-leaf parsley, finely
 chopped
1 garlic clove, finely chopped
8 sprigs of fresh mint, finely
 chopped
3 tablespoons olive oil
salt and freshly ground
 black pepper

serves 4

1 Remove the outer leaves of the artichokes and trim the stalks. Loosen the inner leaves and with a sharp knife remove the choke. Place the prepared artichoke in a bowl of water and lemon juice to prevent discoloration.

2 Mix together the parsley, garlic and mint with enough olive oil to make the mixture wet, then season. Stuff the artichokes with the herb mixture and re-close the leaves as tightly as possible.

3 Snugly fit the artichokes upside-down in a deep earthenware dish. Season well, then fill the dish with one part water and two parts oil, cover the dish with a lid or tinfoil and bake in a preheated oven, 160°C/325°F/gas 3, for about 1 hour. Drain and serve hot or cold.

SAGRA DELLE CILIEGE

THE CHERRY FESTIVAL

Fruit is usually served at the end of most Italian meals, and June marks the appearance on the table of bowls of luscious scarlet cherries.

Many varieties of cherry are grown all over Italy; Vignola in Emilia-Romagna is said to supply most of the cherries eaten in Europe, and its high concentration of trees makes it a very attractive place to visit in spring when the trees are in full bloom and in summer when they are laden with deep red fruit. Maraschino and Amarene cherries, which grow in the south, and the large, dark and sweet Visciole, from which Visner, a special sun-fermented liqueur, is made, are just some of the popular varieties.

Cherry festivals are particularly joyous affairs; cartloads and basketfuls of cherries are taken to the market square and people come from the surrounding villages to buy crates to make enough jams, pickles and preserves to last the winter and to make traditional sweets and cakes such as *dolce amore* (a cake layered with cherry jam, sponge fingers, liqueurs and *zabajon*), and *tortelli di Carnevale* (Carnival pastries).

CROSTATA DI CILIEGE

CHERRY TART

PASTRY
175g plain flour
45g caster sugar
125g chilled butter, cut
   into cubes
1 egg yolk
1 teaspoon vanilla essence

FILLING
1 egg + 1 egg yolk
25g caster sugar
finely grated zest of 1 lemon
25g plain flour
250ml double cream
175g fresh or bottled cherries

serves 6–8

1 First make the pastry. Combine the flour, sugar and butter in a food processor until the mixture resembles breadcrumbs, or rub together with your fingers. Then quickly mix in the egg yolk and vanilla essence. Turn onto a lightly floured surface and knead until smooth. Chill for 20 minutes.

2 Roll out the pastry and line a 24cm loose-bottomed tart tin. Bake blind in a preheated oven, 200°C/400°F/gas 6, for about 15 minutes. Remove from the oven and leave to cool. Turn down the oven to 180°C/350°F/gas 4.

3 To make the filling, whisk the egg, egg yolk, sugar and lemon zest until light and fluffy. Add the flour and mix well, and then add the cream. Pour into the pastry case and arrange the cherries evenly.

4 Bake for about 30 minutes or until set and golden. Allow the tart to stand for a few minutes before lifting it out of the tin and transferring it to a serving dish. Serve warm or cold.

AMARENE AL LIQUORE

CHERRIES PRESERVED IN ALCOHOL

1kg ripe unblemished cherries
1 cinnamon stick
100g caster sugar
200ml good quality rum
bottling alcohol

1 Wash and dry the cherries and pack them tightly in a sterilised jar, adding pieces of the cinnamon stick at regular intervals.

2 Dissolve the sugar in the rum and pour onto the cherries. Fill the jar with the bottling alcohol and seal.

3 Leave the jar in a warm place, possibly in the sun, for two months, shaking and turning it every day. Then store in the pantry until needed.

Il Palio di Siena

The word *palio* has two meanings: it is both a race and a piece of cloth, the cloth being a silk banner awarded to the winner of the race. Many such *palios*, or horse races, take place in Tuscany, the most famous of which is the world-renowned Palio di Siena, held in the town's beautiful Piazza del Campo. Two races are run, on 2nd July and 16th August, but festivities start as early as 27th May, when in the Palazzo Comunale (the town hall) the order of the horses is established by a public draw. From then on all sorts of ritual celebrations take place: the horses are blessed in their own parishes, a trial race is run, costume parades, flag-throwing competitions, and banquets and dances are organised. It is an important festival for the locals and a privileged spectacle for visitors. All who attend will eat heartily of Tuscany's cuisine, not least a piece of Siena's famous Panforte.

right The Palio, Siena; Simeone Huber/Stone/ Getty Images

PANFORTE
di SIENA

In the *Divine Comedy* Dante refers to Niccolo' Salimbeni, a native of Siena, who brought back from one of his trips to the Orient 'honeyed and peppered breads', and it is from this that Panforte is said to have developed. Traditionally a Christmas treat, it can now be bought all year round.

200g blanched almonds,
  finely chopped
115g walnuts, finely chopped
115g dried figs, finely chopped
170g candied peel, finely
  chopped
1 teaspoon ground cinnamon
1 teaspoon mixed spice
170g honey
85g caster sugar
2–4 sheets rice paper

1 In a large bowl combine the nuts, figs, peel, cinnamon and mixed spice.

2 Warm the honey in a saucepan over a medium heat and, as it becomes runny, add the sugar and stir until dissolved. Do not let it boil. Pour over the nuts and spices and mix well.

3 Line the bottom of a 20cm loose-bottomed cake tin with the rice paper and pour the mixture in; smooth out the surface and cover with the remaining rice paper, or sprinkle with flour and a little cinnamon.

4 Bake in a preheated oven, 180°C/350°F/gas 4, for about 30 minutes. Leave to cool in the cake ring for 10 minutes, and then take out of the tin and leave to go cold on a cooling rack.

5 Store in an airtight tin. Panforte is better eaten one or two days after baking. If you sprinkled it with flour, remove the excess with a pastry brush before storing.

SAGRA DELL' Olio d'Oliva

FESTIVAL OF OLIVE OIL

The olive is the one single ingredient that distinguishes Italian cooking from any other style. Olives grow in almost all regions of Italy, and yield the best extra virgin oil in the world. Each region grows a different variety of tree and produces a different-tasting olive, from the slightly peppery taste of Tuscan olives to the sweeter, more delicate taste of Liguria oil and the almost perfumed southern oil. The olives are harvested in November and December either by hand-picking the fallen olives or by stretching sheets under the trees and then beating or shaking the branches. Within a week of harvesting, the olives will be crushed and the oil squeezed from the pulp in special oil presses.

Oil festivals are celebrated in the late summer, to which producers bring samples of the past harvest for everyone to taste, and of course speculate on the serious matter of the new harvest. Oil is usually tasted on bread, though the experts need only rub a few drops into the warmth of the palm of their hands. While these antics go on, seasonal local specialities will be on offer with great quantities of wine, so that discussions can stretch into the evening.

left Olive trees; Brendan Walker/Iconica/Getty Images

Bruschetta

The tradition of bruschetta goes back to the Romans, who ate it in great quantities with *mulsum* (honeyed wine) at such festivals as the Saturnalia. The tradition of Bruschetta Festivals continues to this day in some villages. In Spello, Umbria, the Sagra della Bruschetta takes place at the beginning of February and the oil used at this time will still be fresh from the pressing, adding special character to this dish.

To make bruschetta all you need is a good round loaf of country-style Italian bread, cut in thick slices. Either grill, toast or colour it on a barbecue, and as soon as the bread starts to crisp remove from the heat, rub with a cut clove of garlic and sprinkle generously with extra virgin olive oil. Serve as an appetiser on its own or with slices of plum tomatoes and mozzarella, or instead of croûtons in a salad or as an accompaniment to a hearty soup.

Pinzimonio

OLIVE OIL DRESSING

Virgin olive oil is the perfect dip for fresh raw vegetables; simply season with salt and freshly ground black pepper, and add a little lemon juice or vinegar if you like. Though this is a rustic way of serving vegetables, it can make an elegant first course for a summer lunch with carefully chosen vegetables such as crispy white fennel, juicy peppers and ripe plum tomatoes.

right Revello Family Olive Farm, Riviera di Ponente; SIME/Corbis

SAGRA DELL' AGLIO

GARLIC FESTIVAL

Garlic is usually associated with the cooking of south Italy, and indeed it is widely used there in soups, and with fish and vegetables, but many northern recipes also make use of it. In the villages of Molino dei Torti, in Piedmont, and Vessolico, in Liguria, the garlic harvest is celebrated at the end of July or the beginning of August. Here, as in many other villages where garlic is grown and fêted, the crops are taken to the market square for a particularly fragrant selling and buying session. Farmers have distinctive ways of plaiting their garlic stalks and for this occasion elaborate structures of tresses, garlands and wreaths are used as white perfumed decorations to embellish the stalls. Many people take this chance to stock up with this useful ingredient. Not surprisingly, plenty of wine will be at hand to quench the thirst but also to help reduce some of the aroma left in the mouth by various tastings of garlicky bruschettas and crostini.

left Fresh garlic; Roy Morsch/zefa/Corbis

BAGNA CAODA

HOT ANCHOVY SAUCE

This is a traditional Piedmontese dish. Bagna Caoda means 'hot sauce', and it is served in a terracotta saucepan set over a flame and kept bubbling throughout the meal. Raw and blanched vegetables are dipped in the sauce and sometimes thin strips of raw beef are added. Anchovies and garlic are the most important ingredients in this recipe; for a very creamy end result use two or three times the amount of garlic suggested below and marinate the cloves in milk overnight; add the butter and simmer until the garlic is completely soft, then proceed with the recipe.

115g butter
6 garlic cloves, peeled and sliced
140g anchovy fillets
200ml olive oil
4–5 walnuts, chopped (optional)
fresh vegetables for dipping:
    fennel, peppers, cauliflower
    florets, roasted onions, leaves
    of Savoy cabbage, sliced and
    boiled Jerusalem artichokes,

serves 4

1 Gently heat the butter and garlic in an earthenware saucepan, and leave to simmer until the garlic is soft; take care not to let it burn.

2 Add the anchovies to the softened garlic and mix until they have amalgamated sufficiently.

3 Stir in the oil and walnuts and heat through.

FERRAGOSTO

Ferragosto falls during August, the hottest month of the year, when the Italians take their holidays, and shops and offices are closed. The name derives from Feriae Augustae, a festival declared to celebrate the emperor Augustus on the first day of the month named after him. Many other Roman festivals were celebrated during August, including one in honour of a god of abundance, Ops, from whose name is derived the word 'opulence'. Nowadays the August festival of Ferragosto is celebrated on the 15th; the day in the Christian calendar AD 45 when it is believed the Virgin Mary ascended to Heaven.

This combination of pagan and religious history is typical of many Italian festivals; though it represents for many a day of rest and fun it is mixed with reverence and respect for the Virgin Mary. As many churches are dedicated to her this day becomes a special feast day in many villages. Statues are taken in procession along the main streets before being returned to the church and blessed; and villagers can then fall to more earthly enjoyment in the shape of food and wine.

More generally, it is a day to forget about work, to eat, drink and be merry, and many people choose to escape the towns and cities to the coast, to eat in style, sampling festive and regional dishes in the many restaurants and resorts, or in the peace and quiet of the countryside with a picnic.

left Bronze head of Augustus; Sandro Vannini/Corbis

BOMBA DI RISO
ALLA PIACENTINA

RICE 'BOMBE' PIACENZA-STYLE

1 small onion, finely chopped
115g butter
1 large pigeon, cleaned
   and boned
2 tablespoons dry white wine
400g tin of plum tomatoes,
   drained and chopped
3 fresh sage leaves,
   finely chopped
550g Arborio or pudding rice
4 tablespoons grated parmesan
2 eggs
4–5 tablespoons dried
   breadcrumbs
salt and freshly ground
   black pepper

1 Sweat the onion in half the butter for a few minutes, then add the pieces of boned pigeon and leave to colour.

2 Deglaze with the wine, add the tomatoes and sage, and season. Simmer for about 10 minutes, remove and keep warm.

3 Cook the rice in boiling salted water until al dente, drain, rinse with cold water and drain again.

4 Stir into the rice the sauce, the remaining butter (save a few pieces for dotting the top), the parmesan and the eggs.

5 Grease an ovenproof dish, preferably a bowl, and line with two thirds of the breadcrumbs. Arrange two thirds of the rice mixture in the bowl. Make a well in the centre; into this put the pigeon, cover with the remaining rice, sprinkle with breadcrumbs and dot with a few pieces of butter.

6 Bake in a preheated oven, 180°C/350°F/gas 4, for about 45 minutes or until golden and crunchy on top. Remove from the oven, leave to stand for about 10 minutes and then turn out onto a serving plate.

ARISTA ALLA FIORENTINA

ROAST LOIN
OF PORK FLORENCE-STYLE

Some date the origin of this dish to 1430 when a group of Greek bishops attended an ecumenical council in Florence called by Pope Eugenius IV. Roast loin of pork was served at one of the banquets and was quickly dubbed *aristos* (the best) by one of the bishops... and the name stuck. Others say it comes from the Latin *arista* (top part), in this case the saddle.

This roast is often cooked on a spit but when roasting in the oven use the fat released during cooking to roast potatoes to be served with the meat.

2 garlic cloves
3–4 sprigs of rosemary
1.5kg loin of pork, boned,
   rolled and tied
salt and freshly ground
   black pepper

serves 6

1 Chop the garlic and rosemary together. Make small incisions in the fat of the roast and rub in the garlic and rosemary. Season well.

2 Roast in a preheated oven, 190°C/375°F/gas 5, for about 1½ hours, basting and turning the meat occasionally.

GELO DI MELONE

WATERMELON JELLY

This is a traditional dish made in Palermo in Sicily for Ferragosto; a lemon and a jasmine version are also made for this occasion.

1 ripe watermelon, weighing
　　about 5kg
700g caster sugar
250g arrowroot or potato starch
1 teaspoon vanilla essence
100g bitter chocolate, chopped
100g candied fruit, chopped
30g pistachios, peeled and
　　finely chopped
ground cinnamon

serves 6–8

1 Remove the pulp from the watermelon and pass it through a sieve. Add the sugar and arrowroot or starch.

2 Gently heat the melon mix, and then simmer for a few minutes. Remove from heat and stir in the vanilla essence. Leave to cool.

3 When it's almost cold mix in the chocolate, candied fruit and pistachios. Pour into wet individual moulds or into one large mould and leave to set in the fridge for at least 2–3 hours (preferably overnight).

4 Turn onto serving plates and sprinkle with cinnamon.

Sagra Delle Cozze e Pesce

FESTIVAL OF MUSSELS AND FISH

The Mediterranean shores of Italy offer a wide variety of fish and shellfish, and coastal towns and villages boast spectacular fish markets. One such fishing centre is Taranto, which celebrates during September a feast in honour of Stella Maris (the Star of the Sea), who is said to protect the fishermen when out in their boats. Blessed with ideal conditions to raise shellfish, Taranto has been famous since its first Spartan settlers in 706 BC for its clams, mussels, sea urchins and oysters (including the ones used to produce the purple dye of Roman emperors' togas). It is still the principal supplier to the rest of Italy. Because of the high quality of the fish, locals tend to eat raw fish fresh from the sea, bought from the long line of fish stalls along the seafront selling the catch of the day. But during the festivities special barbecue fires are lit on the seafront and fish is grilled or fried and consumed in the open as the boats return; large quantities of mussels, clams and oysters are offered, so that everyone has a chance to enjoy what is considered the pride of the town.

left A Marina, Campania; Simeone Huber/Photographer's Choice/Getty Images

Cozze Ripiene al Sugo

STUFFED MUSSELS IN TOMATO SAUCE

1kg large mussels, washed
  and scrubbed
75ml olive oil
2 garlic cloves
400g tin plum tomatoes,
  chopped
sprig of basil, chopped
bunch of flat-leaf parsley,
  chopped
2 eggs
3–4 tablespoons dried
  breadcrumbs
salt and freshly ground
  black pepper

serves 4

1 With a sharp knife open each mussel without separating the two valves. Wash well in salted water and drain.

2 To make the sauce, heat the oil in a saucepan and add 1 garlic clove; leave to flavour the oil and remove as it starts to colour. Add the tomatoes, a little water (the sauce should be sufficient to cover the mussels), and the basil. Season and simmer for 15–20 minutes.

3 For the stuffing, mix together the parsley, eggs, the remaining garlic clove (finely chopped) and enough breadcrumbs to make a moist mixture.

4 Stuff each mussel with the mixture, close the two valves and tie with sewing thread. Add the mussels to the tomato sauce and simmer for 15–20 minutes.

5 Untie the mussels and serve hot with rice or pasta.

Frittura di Cozze

DEEP-FRIED MUSSELS

Serve these mussels as a starter or as appetisers with drinks.

1kg mussels, washed
  and scrubbed
225g plain flour
2 eggs, beaten
250g dried breadcrumbs
olive oil for deep-frying
salt
lemon wedges to serve

serves 4

1 With a sharp knife remove and discard one half of the mussel shell, taking care not to damage the molluscs. Wash the half shells with the mussels in slightly salted water, drain well and pat dry.

2 Toss in the flour, then dip in beaten egg and finally in breadcrumbs.

3 Fry a few mussels at a time in hot oil until golden. Pile on a serving plate, sprinkle with salt and serve with lemon wedges.

CALAMARI SOTT'ACETO

SQUID PRESERVED IN VINEGAR

In Puglia this dish is prepared with octopus. It will be good to eat after only a few days, as an appetiser or as part of a seafood salad.

900g baby squids, cleaned,
  gutted and washed
bunch of fresh mint
4–5 garlic cloves, peeled
  and sliced
white wine vinegar

serves 4

1 Bring a large pot of water to the boil and blanch the baby squid for a few minutes until tender. (If using large squid, skin them and cut them into rounds; they may also need longer cooking.)

2 Drain well and pack into jars, alternating the squid with layers of fresh mint leaves and slices of garlic. Fill the jar with vinegar and seal.

Pesci Fritti All'Agliata

MARINATED FRIED FISH

225g plain flour
900g whole, small fish such as
  sardines, sole, trout,
  gutted and washed
olive oil for frying
sprig each of rosemary, sage
  and oregano
2 garlic cloves, chopped
white wine vinegar
salt and freshly ground
  black pepper

serves 4

1 Season the flour with salt and pepper. Toss the fish in the seasoned flour and shallow-fry in the oil until golden. Arrange in a deep serving dish.

2 Heat 2–3 tablespoons of fresh oil to the pan, and fry the herbs and garlic for a few seconds. Add the vinegar, heat through and pour over the fish.

3 Leave to marinate for a few hours or overnight, and serve cold.

SAGRA DELLE LENTICCHIE

LENTIL FESTIVAL

The best lentils produced in Italy come from Abruzzi, a region rich in culinary traditions. The countryside surrounding the village of Santo Stefano di Sassanio is known for its excellent crop of small, dark lentils, which maintain their shape during the short time needed to cook them and are said to be some of the tastiest in the world. The village celebrates its crop every year during the harvest in late September, when the short flat pods are collected from the bushy lentil plants and gathered in crates and sacks. As the picking is still done by hand the end of the harvest means party time for all those involved. When all the work is finished, growers, villagers and pickers gather together in the main square where the festivities start; and of course lentils find their way onto the menu in the form of a hearty lentil stew eaten with locally produced sausages, pork ribs and plenty of local wine.

right Fields surrounding Santo Stefano di Sassanio;
Paolo Ramazzotti/www.montegeologo.com

ZUPPA DI LENTICCHIE ABRUZZESE

LENTIL SOUP ABRUZZI-STYLE

200g brown lentils, soaked
  overnight and drained
2 bay leaves
100ml olive oil
20 roasted chestnuts, peeled
  and chopped
115g streaky bacon, diced
  (optional)
sprig of thyme
sprig of marjoram
400g tin plum tomatoes,
  chopped
salt and freshly ground
  black pepper
4 large slices of country-style
  bread, thinly cut

serves 4

1 Simmer the lentils with the bay leaves in boiling water until the lentils are tender.

2 Meanwhile heat half the oil in a saucepan, add the chestnuts and bacon if using and fry for a few minutes. Add the thyme and marjoram and then the tomatoes. Season and simmer for 5–10 minutes.

3 Combine the lentils and cooking liquid with the tomato sauce and simmer for a further 10 minutes.

4 Fry the bread slices in the remaining olive oil or grill them and brush them with the oil. Place one slice of bread in each serving bowl and ladle soup over it. Serve immediately with freshly ground black pepper.

LENTICCHIE IN UMIDO

STEWED LENTILS

85g pancetta (Italian bacon),
  diced
1 small onion, chopped
5 sage leaves, chopped
285g brown lentils soaked
  overnight and drained
salt and freshly ground
  black pepper

serves 4

1 Gently heat the pancetta in a saucepan until it starts releasing its fat, then add the onion and sage and fry for a few minutes.

2 Add the lentils and cover with water. Simmer gently for about 1 hour until all the water is absorbed and the lentils are tender. Season and serve.

SAGRA DEL SEDANO D'ORO

FESTIVAL OF THE GOLDEN CELERY

The ancient Romans wore celery wreaths in the belief that celery was a cure for hangovers; they also decorated family tombs with it, and ate it as a dessert, cooked with honey and pepper. Celery is said to be good for your health, and some people claim it has aphrodisiac qualities if eaten raw in large enough quantity. It is certainly

eaten and enjoyed all over Italy, where many varieties are grown. In central and southern Italy the fat, juicy stalks are eaten raw, dipped in Pinzimonio (olive oil dressing), or Tomato Sauce, or as part of a salad; in Liguria it is often eaten with olives, pecorino and crusty bread as an appetiser, and in Friuli a traditional celery soup is served on Christmas Eve.

The best celery is produced in Tuscany and Umbria, and at the end of September the village of Figline Valdarno celebrates the festival of the Sedano d'Oro. All the market stalls make way for baskets of golden celery and each farmer enters his best specimens in the contest for the perfect head of celery.

SEDANI ALLA PRATESE

TUSCAN-STYLE STUFFED CELERY

2 large, tender heads of celery
3 tablespoons olive oil
1 medium onion, chopped
200g chicken livers, cleaned
and chopped
115g each Parma and cooked
ham, finely diced
115g minced veal
200g mushrooms (preferably
wild), chopped
150ml dry white wine
225g plain flour
150ml milk
pinch of grated nutmeg
3 tablespoons grated parmesan
2 eggs, beaten
250g dried breadcrumbs
olive oil for frying
salt and freshly ground
black pepper

1 Strip off the celery stalks, cut them into 7cm pieces and blanch in boiling, lightly salted water. When just tender, refresh in cold water and drain.

2 Heat the olive oil in a saucepan, add the onion and when coloured add the liver, hams, veal and mushrooms. Simmer for a few minutes and then add the white wine.

3 When the wine has almost totally evaporated sprinkle in 1 tablespoon of the flour and stir in the milk, nutmeg and parmesan. Season and cook, stirring continuously, until the mixture has thickened enough to stuff the celery stalks.

4 Remove from the heat and stuff each piece of celery with a little mixture, then toss in the flour, dip in the egg and finally cover with breadcrumbs.

5 Shallow-fry a few pieces at a time until golden. Serve hot.

serves 6

SAGRA DEI FUNGHI E

FESTIVAL OF WILD MUSHROOMS AND TRUFFLES

During the mushroom season from the end of September to November, Italians all over the country begin the serious ritual of mushroom hunting. Rising early in the morning, not only at weekends but sometimes before going to work, they venture into the woods kitted with woven baskets (any other kind of carrier could damage the spoils of the search), walking sticks, short knives and Wellington boots, and the hope of a good catch. Everyone has a favourite place to go and this closely guarded secret is not shared with just anyone but passed from generation to generation (I was shown by my father where my grandparents hunted for ceps and chanterelles). Finding even just one mushroom is an elating experience and there is a magical feeling while hunting, probably because one is walking through the woods in the silence and stillness of the early autumn mist.

During the month of October, towns and villages hold festivals where many varieties of mushrooms are put on show in baskets lined with chestnut or fern leaves. All the edible varieties will be on sale, and the bartering and bargaining is mingled with boastful stories from the more seasoned hunters.

bei Tartufi

behind Hunting for truffles; Dennis Marsico/Corbis

Even the most overfilled basket, however, will be overshadowed by the find of one small truffle. White truffles are particularly sought after and are found only in Italy, particularly around Alba, in Piedmont. The festival the town organises to celebrate the white truffle is attended by international chefs and gourmets and by buyers from all over the world, as well as the locals. Auctions are held for large quantities but individual truffles can be bought from the hunters; and of course wine and other local delicacies are at hand to help along the festivities.

Mushrooms need to be consumed almost immediately and well dried; when possible simply brush off earth deposits or use a damp cloth. Small, firm ceps can be preserved in oil after having been blanched in vinegared water, and served during the winter as an appetiser. Some species can be frozen and then added to soups and stews. Ceps are probably the most versatile and, like morels, can be bought dried all year round.

POLENTA COI FUNGHI

POLENTA WITH WILD MUSHROOM RAGOUT

POLENTA
1½ litres milk
300g maize flour
115g butter
salt and freshly ground
   black pepper

MUSHROOM RAGOUT
70ml olive oil
1 medium onion, finely chopped
3 garlic cloves, finely chopped
550g mixed wild mushrooms,
   cleaned and roughly cut
3 tablespoons dry white wine
115g butter
juice of ½ lemon
2 tablespoons flat-leaf parsley,
   finely chopped
salt and freshly ground
   black pepper

serves 4

1 To make the polenta, heat the milk and season well. When it starts to simmer gradually whisk in the maize flour. Simmer for about 45 minutes, stirring from time to time. Add the butter and mix.

2 To make the ragout, heat the oil in a saucepan, add the onion and garlic, and leave to colour. Add the mushrooms and fry for a few minutes, then add the white wine and a couple of tablespoons of water. Cover and simmer for about 15 minutes.

3 Remove the lid and allow most of the juices to evaporate, then incorporate the butter and lemon juice. Stir in the parsley, check the seasoning and serve immediately with the polenta.

FUNGHI AL FUNGITIELLO

WILD MUSHROOM STEW

Serve with bruschetta or polenta or with roast quails.

75ml olive oil
2 garlic cloves, crushed
1kg mixed wild mushrooms,
  cleaned and roughly cut
400g tin plum tomatoes, chopped
2–3 tablespoons flat-leaf
  parsley, chopped
1 small chilli, seeded and finely
  chopped
salt and freshly ground
  black pepper

serves 4

1 Heat the oil with the garlic; when it starts to sizzle add the mushrooms and fry for a few minutes.

2 Add the tomatoes and leave to simmer for 10–15 minutes until the stew has thickened a little.

3 Add the parsley and chilli, check the seasoning and serve.

CROSTINI AI TARTUFI

TRUFFLE CROÛTONS

1 tablespoon olive oil
115g butter
1 anchovy fillet
⅓ small garlic clove,
   finely chopped
1 teaspoon flat-leaf parsley,
   finely chopped
100g truffles, preferably white,
   finely sliced
4 slices of good white bread,
   crust removed and cut into
   small squares or triangles

serves 4

1 Heat the oil and a third of the butter in a saucepan, add the anchovy, garlic and parsley and leave to simmer for a couple of minutes.

2 Add the truffle slices and leave to infuse over a low heat for about 5 minutes.

3 Meanwhile, fry the croûtons in the remaining butter.

4 Spread a little truffle sauce on each croûton and enjoy.

Risotto Ai Tartufi

TRUFFLE RISOTTO

140g butter
1 small onion, finely chopped
350g arborio rice
100ml dry white wine
1 litre meat or chicken stock
115g grated parmesan
1 small white truffle
salt and freshly ground
  black pepper

serves 4

1 Melt half the butter in a saucepan, add the onion and leave to colour. Add the rice and fry for a couple of minutes.

2 Add the white wine to the rice and simmer to evaporate. Heat the stock separately until simmering and add to the rice, a few ladles at a time, stirring continuously and allowing the stock to be absorbed between additions. The rice should take about 20 minutes to cook and have a creamy texture but each grain should still have bite.

3 Check the seasoning, and add the remaining butter and the parmesan. Cover and leave to stand for a few minutes. Serve sprinkled with truffle shavings.

left Truffle Hunter; David Gallant/Corbis

Sagra delle Castagne

CHESTNUT FESTIVAL

The autumn heralds for children in Italy the beginning of the conker season, and for everyone else the pleasure of roasting chestnuts over open fires in special iron pans with perforated bottoms to allow the flames to scorch the shiny brown skins and make peeling the chestnuts easier.

Many types of chestnut contain three or four nuts in each shell but the best type are those that yield just one or two nuts. Piedmont, Lombardy and Veneto have a great number of chestnut trees, many growing wild, and in these regions villages celebrate the harvest with great bonfires, in which the nuts are roasted. Popular in these regions are autumn chestnut soups, tarts and rich cakes, made with chestnut flour, and from the crops gathered near Aosta a most delicious but extremely rich chestnut cream is made, often used to make Mont Blanc, a concoction of sweet chestnut purée, whipped cream and grated chocolate.

RICE, MILK AND CHESTNUT SOUP

You can use dried chestnuts for this but soak for at least one day before cooking.

200g fresh chestnuts, skinned
2 litres water
salt
140g risotto or pudding rice
500ml milk
30g butter
pinch of ground cinnamon

serves 4

1 Put the chestnuts in a large saucepan and cover with the water. Add salt and bring to the boil. Simmer for around 1½ hours.

2 Add the rice and when the rice is half cooked incorporate the milk and butter. Simmer until the soup has reached a creamy consistency. Serve hot sprinkled with a little cinnamon.

CHESTNUTS BERGAMO-STYLE

1kg hot roasted chestnuts
70ml Grappa (eau de vie)
2–3 tablespoons caster sugar

serves 4–5

1 Quickly peel the chestnuts while still hot. Toss them dry in a frying pan (do not use any butter or oil) over a high heat.

2 Remove from heat and sprinkle with the Grappa and the sugar. Quickly mix and flambé (the heated spirit will light with a match). Eat as soon as the flames disappear.

FESTA DEI MORTI

ALL SOULS' DAY

The tradition of remembering the dead dates from prehistoric times, and all cultures have some form of ritual to express respect and veneration towards deceased loved ones. In the Christian calendar the first two days of November are set aside for the commemoration of the dead: 1st November is All Saints' Day, a Holy day of Obligation when all the saints who are not celebrated on any particular day during the year are remembered and prayed to; 2nd November is All Souls' Day, commemorating all the faithful departed, and on this day of mourning and rejoicing families visit the graves of their loved ones, bringing flowers and wreaths. Italians maintain strong family ties, and this celebration is a deeply felt one. At one time offerings of food would be left on the graves, and from this derives the tradition of leaving small breads, sweets, beans and lentils on the kitchen table at night with the windows ajar to allow the dead to enter, see the offerings and hear the prayers said in their honour. This custom is still practised in some southern villages.

Special cakes are eaten at this time, and biscuits made in the form of broad beans, Fave dei Morti, an association dating back to Egyptian times, when it was believed that the beans contained the souls of loved ones.

right San Miniato churchyard with Florence in the background; Michael Pasdzior/The Image Bank/Corbis

BREAD FOR THE DEAD

Serve these biscuits with coffee, or a sweet white wine.

450g Amaretti biscuits, ground
285g caster sugar
225g plain flour
115g ground almonds
1 teaspoon baking powder
1 teaspoon ground cinnamon
115g sultanas, soaked in
   warm water
115g dried figs, chopped
4 egg whites
70ml dry white wine
4–5 sheets of rice paper
icing sugar for sprinkling

makes 20–25

1 Mix together all the dry ingredients. Drain the sultanas and add them witht the figs.

2 Make a well in the centre and add the egg whites and enough white wine to form a dough. Knead vigorously for about 10 minutes.

3 Shape the dough into small, flat elongated breads and place each on to a piece of rice paper.

4 Bake in a preheated oven, 180°C/350°F/gas 4, for about 20–25 minutes, until the breads are dry all the way through. Cool, sprinkle with icing sugar and serve. They can be eaten immediately or stored for a few days in an airtight container.

VIGILIA DI NATALE

CHRISTMAS EVE

Christmas Eve in Italy is spent, as in many other countries, with the family, adding the last few touches to the Christmas tree – coloured lights, glass balls, streamers, mandarin oranges and sweets or pieces of *torrone* (nougat) in decorative boxes. In preparation for the feasting of Christmas Day, and as a sign of respect for the Body of Christ, Christmas Eve is a *giorno di magro* (a lean day) and no meat is consumed. In most households fish will be served for lunch and dinner, and in central and southern Italy this is likely to be eel, either as a main course or as part of a rice or pasta dish.

Fettucini con la Mollica

FETTUCINI WITH DRIED BREADCRUMBS

PASTA
200g plain flour
pinch of salt
2 eggs
140g semolina

SAUCE
100ml olive oil
1 small garlic clove
5 anchovy fillets
½ small chilli, seeded and
    chopped (optional)
90g dried breadcrumbs
salt and freshly ground
    black pepper

serves 4

1 First make the pasta. Sift the flour and salt onto a clean, dry working surface, make a well in the centre and break the eggs into it. Gently mix to form a dough and knead for about 10–15 minutes until the dough is smooth and fairly dry. Cover and leave to rest in a cool place for about 15 minutes.

2 Divide the dough into six pieces and roll out thinly, using either a rolling pin or a pasta machine. Leave the pasta sheets to dry for a few minutes.

3 Cut into thin strips by rolling up each sheet and with a sharp knife cutting across the roll. Unroll the strips and toss in the semolina (the semolina absorbs excess moisture and speeds up the drying of the pasta).

4 Cook the pasta in boiling salted water for 3–4 minutes, taking care not to overdo it.

5 While the pasta is cooking, heat half the oil in a saucepan with the garlic clove; as soon as it starts to colour remove it, add the anchovies and cook gently to allow the anchovies to dissolve. Add the chilli if using.

6 Drain the pasta and dress with the remaining olive oil and the anchovy sauce. Toss well, season, sprinkle with breadcrumbs and serve immediately.

PANETTONE

The name of this cake is said to come from a Milanese baker Antonio (Toni), who concocted it to impress a girlfriend around Christmas time in the fifteenth century; the result was so successful not just with the girl but with many of his other clients that 'Pan de Toni' became a regular feature in the Christmas season.

25g fresh yeast
150ml lukewarm milk
400g plain flour
1 egg
2 egg yolks
45g caster sugar
1 teaspoon vanilla essence
170g butter, melted
85g candied fruit, chopped
85g sultanas
zest of 1 orange, finely grated

1 Cream the yeast in a small bowl with 2 tablespoons of the warm milk. Add 2 tablespoons of the flour and a pinch of sugar, mix to a batter, cover and leave to foam in a warm place (approximately 30 minutes).

2 Beat the egg and egg yolks with the sugar, vanilla essence and two thirds of the melted butter.

3 Sift the flour into a warm bowl, and mix together the yeast mixture and egg mixture. Make a well in the centre of the flour and pour in the yeast and egg mixture, and then the remaining warm milk. Knead until you have a smooth, shiny dough. Grease a clean bowl, place the dough in it, cover and leave to prove in a warm place for about 1–2 hours, until doubled in size.

4 Turn the dough onto a lightly floured surface and knead for about 5 minutes more. Leave to prove again until doubled in volume.

5 Meanwhile, prepare a 15cm tin at least 7.5cm deep; tie a foil collar around it to double its depth to 15cm. Gently grease the tin and foil, and line the bottom of the tin with greased greaseproof paper.

6 Knock back the dough after the second proving and incorporate the candied fruit, sultanas and zest.

7 Shape into a ball, place in the prepared tin and with a sharp knife score the top. Bake in a preheated oven, 200°C/400°F/gas 6, for 10 minutes, then brush with the remaining melted butter, lower the heat to 180°C/350°F/gas 4 and bake for a further 45 minutes or until a skewer inserted in the middle comes out dry.

8 Leave the panettone to stand for 5 minutes before removing the collar and lifting out of the tin. Serve cold.

NATALE

CHRISTMAS

Christmas is very much a family feast in Italy. As in countries the world over, the early morning is a time for the children, for the race to the tree or the *presepio* (the crib) to see and open the presents. Savouring a glass of good Prosecco (an Italian dry sparkling wine) or uncorking a vintage bottle are left to the older generations, and the ritual of preparing the festive table and the celebratory meal is a joint effort enjoyed by all. Friends and relatives drop in to exchange presents and good wishes, and sweet niblets are prepared to welcome them: nougat, nuts, spicy biscuits and, my favourite, plump figs stuffed with nuts and peel and then dipped in chocolate, a speciality of southern Italy.

There is no fixed standard Christmas meal, as each region serves its best produce; the greatest regional influence will be reflected in the antipasti (appetisers), which will include anything from Parma ham, Bresaola (cured fillet of beef), preserved mushrooms, olives to pickled vegetables and fish. Stuffed pasta is usually served as a first course, either in the shape of ravioli or tortellini, which are said to have been offered as Christmas gifts to priests and monks during the twelfth century. A roast will follow, most often some kind of bird, turkey in Lombardy and capon in central Italy, but always accompanied by potatoes, vegetables and salads. The traditional end to the meal is now almost always Panettone, served warm with a glass of sparkling wine or stuffed with ice cream, mascarpone or ricotta, and some regions also serve traditional home-made cakes rich in candied fruits, sultanas and raisins.

right Christmas mass at St Peter's Basilica; Vittoriano Rastelli/Corbis

PIEDMONTESE RAVIOLI

Agnolotti are often poached in meat stock and served like a soup; they can also be dressed with the sauce from a roast or with a light tomato sauce.

PASTA
550g plain flour
3 eggs

FILLING
400g cooked roast beef,
   finely minced
285g Italian sausages, cooked
   and minced
1kg spinach, blanched
   and chopped
pinch of nutmeg
4–5 tablespoons grated parmesan
3–4 eggs, beaten
salt and freshly ground
   black pepper
225g butter
5 sage leaves, chopped

serves 6–8

1 Make the pasta dough following the instructions for fettucine, on page 85. Cover the dough and leave in a cool place while preparing the stuffing.

2 In a bowl mix together the minced beef, sausages, spinach, nutmeg, parmesan and enough egg to hold the stuffing together. Season.

3 Roll out one piece of dough at a time into a thin sheet and place little balls of stuffing at 5cm intervals on the pasta. Roll out another sheet of dough and place on top of stuffing, pressing the two sheets together. If the dough is too dry to seal well, brush the under sheet with egg wash. Cut into squares with a pastry cutter. Place the agnolotti on kitchen cloths dusted with flour and continue until all the dough and filling are used up.

4 Bring a large pot of salted water to the boil, lower the heat and cook the agnolotti in simmering water for about 8 minutes. Drain well.

5 Heat the butter and sage in a frying pan until it starts to colour, pour over the pasta and serve immediately, sprinkled with a little extra parmesan.

CAPPONE RIPIENO

STUFFED CAPON

1 capon, weighing about 1.1kg
  (or use guinea fowl instead)
285g each veal and lean
  beef, minced
115g cooked ham, finely diced
115g Parma ham, finely diced
115g mortadella (Italian salami),
  finely diced
100ml Marsala
4 egg whites
4 hard-boiled egg yolks
50ml olive oil
115g butter
salt and freshly ground
  black pepper

serves 4

1 Taking care not to rip the skin, remove the breast from the boned capon, cut into thin strips and set aside.

2 Mix together the veal, beef, hams and mortadella, add the Marsala and egg whites, season and mix well.

3 Stuff the capon with the mixture, placing at regular intervals strips of the breast and quarters of the hard-boiled yolks. Reshape the bird and sew the back with thread or tie neatly.

4 Place on a roasting tray, sprinkle with the oil and dot with the butter, and roast in a preheated oven, 180°C/350°F/ gas 4, for about 1½ hours. Leave to stand for at least 15 minutes before carving.

left Culatelli di Zibello, Parma ham produced by only 12 farmers in Parma;
Bob Sacha/Corbis